LISBURN

An Illustrated History and Companion

Paintings by
Jack Calderwood

Text by
Trevor Neill

Cottage
Publications

First published by Cottage Publications,
Donaghadee, N. Ireland 1996.
Copyrights Reserved.
© Illustrations by Jack Calderwood 1996
© Text by Trevor Neill 1996

Printed in Singapore.

ISBN 1 900935 02 3

List of Contents

The Artist

Jack Calderwood's formative years as an artist were spent as a pupil of one of Northern Ireland's great artists, John Luke, at the Belfast College of Art. On graduation he embarked on a career in the decorative glass business and, as the founder of the Caldermac Studio, there are few parts of the province which have not been enriched by Jack's stained glass work for which he has been elected a fellow of the British Society of Master Glass Painters.

Since his retirement he has found time to explore other media where his natural artistic flair has shone through to bring him prizes in several competitions and recognition through being selection to exhibit at the Royal Ulster Academy Exhibition.

The Author

A Lisburn man born and bred, Trevor Neill has lived most of his life at his picturesque home at Magheralave. Now retired from the civil service where he worked for the Department of Agriculture, Trevor is now able to devote considerable time to local history which has long been his great interest. He is currently a member of the Living Linen Project which is gathering an oral history of the senior management in the 20th century Irish linen industry. He also takes an active interest in Lisburn Historical Society in which he currently holds the post of Hon. Treasurer and he has been a regular contributor of local history articles to the society's journal.

Land of Linen and the Lambeg Drum

The first settlers in Ireland arrived at least 6000 years ago. At that time the Lagan Valley was densely wooded from the valley floor to the piedmont and thus settlement would have been sparse. However at Ballynahatty, on the lower reaches of the River Lagan, five miles from Lisburn, there is the great man-made earthwork of the Giant's Ring. Other associated structures could be seen nearby until around one hundred and fifty years ago, but the spread of farming has erased them. It is thought that the Giant's Ring was constructed around 2000 B.C., so there must have been a reasonably structured society in the area by then.

From 600 A.D. raths or ring forts began to be constructed and all around Lisburn there are numerous examples. By the 9th or 10th century the O'Neills had established a major fort in what is now Castle Gardens and it is thought that the name of Lisnagarvey is derived from the Gaelic name of this fort 'Lios na gleanbhach' which translates as 'fort of the gamblers'. It is believed by some that there was another fort going by the name of 'Lisburn' about the top of the present Hill Street. With the English settlement in the 17th century and the settlers' difficulty in pronouncing Irish names, it was a question of ease of pronunciation that changed the town's name from Lisnagarvey to Lisburn.

The next significant group to leave their mark on the area were the Normans who came to Ireland in 1169. As they gradually built settlements across the country they established lines of communication, with mottes at strategic intervals similar to Duneight just outside Ravernet. Other examples can be found at Edenderry and Dunmurry.

By the early 14th century Norman power was waning and the powers of Irish chieftains had a brief recovery. Lisnagarvey or Lisburn was under the control of the O'Neills, but after Queen Elizabeth's Irish Wars and The Flight of the Earls in 1607 there arose a new power, the 'New English', who arrived during the Plantation of Ulster. Lisburn, with a sizeable part of South Antrim, passed to Sir Fulk Conway by Letter Patent in 1609. It is interesting to note that the Conways' forebears were Normans who, before that, were Vikings settling in the Seine Basin. So these people's travels in some ways mirrored the footsteps of previous settlers, many of whom they were now displacing.

This period of the early 17th century saw the foundation of Lisburn as we know it today. By and large the Lagan Valley at that time was very sparsely populated, and the new settlers that Conway encouraged to come, had to clear the natural forest from the valley floor and surrounding hills. Between the years 1600 and 1641 a great change took place in the appearance of the area, which had been so thickly wooded that it was said "A man might almost make his way from McArt's Fort to Lisnagarvagh on the tops of trees". By 1640, a shortage of fuel was being experienced at local ironworks so the deforestation must have been considerable as the natural woodland gave way to a cultivated landscape.

Naturally the arrival of the new settlers caused great resentment among those already living in the area. This resulted in the rising of 1641, which for a time stopped the constructive work of Chichester (the Crown's representative) and his associates. The rising, which commenced so suddenly, spread over the greater part of Ulster and fortunate indeed were those areas which escaped destruction. Lisburn suffered greatly and Lisburn Museum has an early watercolour by Thomas Robinson showing an overview of the town from Largymore which clearly depicts a memorial to those of the town who lost their lives in this rebellion. The war in Ireland dragged on for a period of twelve years and it was not until September 1653 that Parliament was able to declare it "appeased and ended". The whole period of the

Commonwealth was one of great depression, due partly to external circumstances and partly to the state of devastation in which the country had been left by the rebellion. The letters which were written by Sir George Rawdon to Lord Conway at this time give a fair picture of the condition of the province as a whole. In a letter on 6th November 1657 Rawdon wrote "Some people who had leases are petitioning to give them up, having no money to pay the rent. You cannot think what misery is caused here by the ryalls...corn and cattle bring in nothing, any trade there is, is in butter." An additional problem of the time was a widespread cattle disease which, given the description, was possibly 'foot and mouth disease'. This restricted export of Irish cattle into England, and losses of cattle in the Lisburn area were considerable.

The depression continued after the Restoration, though during the reign of Charles II conditions slowly improved. These improving economic conditions encouraged the noble Lords Hill (of Hillsborough) and Conway to devote money to improvements on their estates.

The death of Charles II in 1685 brought new troubles for the Protestant population of Ulster. The new King James II was a Roman Catholic and he was represented in Ireland by Richard Talbot, Earl of Tirconnell. Tirconnell made no secret of his intention to confiscate all the lands of the English settlers and so great was the alarm that many in the southern part of the country sold their property for what it would fetch and fled to England or Scotland. However Tirconnell's policy at the time did not extend to the north and the lands and estates around Lisburn remained intact.

The end of the period of unrest was at hand however, and with the advent of William III the Presbyterians and Anglicans buried their differences and joined together in support of the new King. For a time the army of King James had control of the Province (except

Derry and Enniskillen) but the arrival of an army under the Duke of Schomberg in 1689 brought matters to a head. Initially Schomberg moved south and confronted the army of James at Dundalk in the Autumn of 1689, but the action ended in stalemate, largely due to the appaling weather. Casualties were high due to inadequate supplies, poor conditions and the fact that many in the armies were inexperienced troops. Schomberg retreated north and those who could march came back largely to the Lisburn area, where Schomberg made his headquarters at No. 11 Castle Street. The sick and wounded were brought back by sea from Dundalk Bay to Belfast Lough where a military hospital was set up in the Strandtown area in East Belfast.

A large portion of the army was quartered at Blaris (which incidentally had served as an army camp as far back as 1004 when Brian Boru had camped his army there) and a part of the cavalry were in the area between Sprucefield and Ravernet, known to this day as Troopersfield. Others were at Glenavy where two squadrons of the Queen's Regiment were quartered. In return for the kindness and hospitality accorded to all ranks by the warm-hearted people of the parish, the officers presented the church with a silver chalice which continues in use on special occasions until this day. The chalice bears the inscription 'This plate was given to ye Church of Glenavy by the Officers of ye Queens Regiment of Horse, commanded by ye Honourable Major General Sir John Lanier, in the year 1690. In honorem Ecclessiae Anglicanae'.

Other units were at Ballinderry, Derriaghy and Drumbo and some soldiers remains are buried in the Cathedral Churchyard and in Derriaghy churchyard. Amongst them is the Duke of Schomberg's pastry cook who died of food poisoning!

The extended billeting around Lisburn over the winter of 1689-90 and its effect on the soldiers' spiritual well-being obviously concerned their commanders because Schomberg sent to London for ministers of the Christian faith. He was sent four amongst whom was one William Doubourdieu who went on with the army for the rest of its Irish campaign but then returned to the Lisburn area where his descendants are still living.

The subsequent arrival of King William himself resulted in the relief of Ulster and in the ultimate defeat of James in 1690. King William spent a brief time in Lisburn on 19th June 1690 and dined with his senior officers in the house of William Edmundson, which stood on the site now occupied by the Northern Bank.

An interesting incident occurred during the Royal Visit involving a Lisburn Presbyterian minister, the Rev. Alex McCracken. With two others he had, some months before, been chosen to go to London with an address of welcome to His Majesty King William. The Rev. McCracken called on His Majesty during the short stay in Lisburn and was received with geniality. Later the same day the Rev. McCracken with the Rev Patrick Adair and other ministers awaited on the King at Hillsborough, who in consequence of their petition, promised to increase the amount of the Regium Donum to twelve hundred pounds per annum.

Another story from this time tells of King William stopping in Lambeg at the blacksmith's forge, where the blacksmith was standing at the door with his pretty wife and two children to see the soldiers go past. However the soldiers were unsure of the road and William himself stopped to ask the blacksmith the right road. His Majesty asked his question in English with a strong French accent but to the astonishment of the company the blacksmith replied in French! The blacksmith's name was Rene Bulmer and he had fled France to escape persecution and made his new home in Lambeg. A house on Church Hill, Lambeg, is believed to be Rene Bulmer's house and Rene is buried in the nearby Lambeg churchyard as are many of his descendants. The christian name Rene is still used in the family although, through time, the surname has altered slightly from Bulmer to Boomer.

The Bulmer family were in fact one of a number of Huguenot families who had arrived in the area around the latter end of the 17th century. The Huguenots, who were French Protestants, had been leaving France because they were not allowed freedom of worship. From the latter part of the 16th century and all through the 17th century, families and groups of these people had been leaving France and moving to Holland, some further into Europe, others coming to England and Ireland, all seeking religious freedom.

The Huguenots in and around Lisburn were augmented by Louis Crommelin and the families brought over by him from France and Holland when the government entered into a contract with him in 1700. He was to invest £10,000 in machinery, looms and bleach-works in preparing flax and in giving instruction. In return the government would pay him interest of 8% on his outlay as well as a salary of £300 per year. The government undertook to maintain three assistants and a minister for the Huguenot colony. Crommelin established a bleachgreen at Hilden which was eventually taken over by another Huguenot family, the Delacherois. They in turn sold it to William Barbour and it is the site of the present threadworks which has been there since 1812.

The Lisburn colony was the only Huguenot colony in the north of Ireland that had a French church. It was situated on the north side of Castle Street, partly on the site of the Town Hall and partly on the site of what, until recently, was Dunnes Stores. One of its more outstanding ministers was the Rev. Saumarez Dubourdieu who was also the vicar of the Parish of Glenavy and, for fifty-six years, Master of the Classical School of Lisburn. His pupils erected a monument to him (a rare event) in 1814 which today can be found on the southside interior of Lisburn Cathedral. The congregation closed about 1820 and they, in literal terms, walked across the street and joined the Cathedral congregation where descendants still worship today. After the congregation had left the church, it served as a town prison and then as a court-house until it was demolished in the early 1880s.

Despite the investments and prosperity brought by the Huguenots, the early 1700s brought disaster and destruction when, in 1707, the town of Lisburn was accidentally burnt. The following brief account was made by the Rev. Joseph Wilkins, Rector, in the Cathedral Register;

> "Memoranda on the 20th day of April 1707, the town of Lisburn, with the church and castle were consumed by an accidental fire"

The fire started on a Sunday while people were in church and before it was extinguished the town had been destroyed. A reminder of this event was recorded on a stone which was set in the wall of the premises adjoining the Assembly Rooms, (though it now resides in the Lisburn Museum) which reads:-

IHI 1708
The year above this house erected
The town was burnt ye year before
People therein may be directed
God hath judgements still in store
And that they do not him provoke
To give to them a second stroke
The builders also doth desire at expiration of his lease
The landlord living at that time may think
Upon the builders case.

The premises at that time were occupied by a Mr. Ward and were the first erected after the fire. The Museum has a watercolour showing the houses, the Assembly Rooms and Market House prior to Sir Richard Wallace's renovations in the late 1880s and this probably gives a good indication of their appearance after the rebuilding. Subsequent alterations in the 19th and 20th centuries have changed the appearance of the buildings as they were developed from dwellings to shops and further into shops and offices.

As the 18th century progressed, and in general was peaceful, trade prospered. The domestic linen industry was no longer domestic as it was exporting ever increasing amounts of its growing output. The once great Irish wool trade had diminished due to tariffs, introduced after the English wool merchants petitioned Parliament at Westminster that the Irish trade was effectively undercutting them. As a sop to the Irish, encouragement was given to the growing of flax and the production of linen as an alternative and thus were sown the seeds of the industry which was to dominate Lisburn as it did many towns throughout Ulster.

By the middle of the 18th century a possibility that had exercised the minds of merchants and engineers was the joining of Belfast with Lough Neagh. The canalisation of the River Lagan was considered the possible answer. With the Lagan at Moira and Lough Neagh just five miles apart over reasonably level terrain, a canal link here had long been proposed. However it took the discovery and exploitation of coal deposits in east Tyrone and the construction of the Newry and Coalisland canals between 1730 and 1742 to give the necessary impetus to get the canal underway. In October 1753 the Irish House of Commons passed an Act 'for making the river Lagan navigable and opening a passage by water between Lough Neagh and the Town of Belfast'.

Next was the monetary problem and, although limited funds were made available by Parliament, to raise the necessary cash, a duty on ale and spirits was levied. It was one penny a gallon on ale and four pence a gallon on spirits manufactured or sold, 'within that part of the district of Lisburn commonly known and distinguished by the gaugers walks of Belfast, Lisburn, Moira and Hillsborough'. The levy was less than enthusiastically received in some quarters and there is a story told about the distillery at Culcavey whose owners, rather than pay the levy, broke the barrels of whiskey and let them flow into the river that flows by way of 'blind man's quay', alongside the Maze racecourse and into the River Lagan. Today this small river is still known locally as the 'whiskey river'.

Construction of the Belfast-Lisburn section of the canal began in 1756 and work brought it up to near Sprucefield by 1763, when further construction ceased for a period due to lack of funds. In spite of this, The Belfast Newsletter of 9th September 1763 had a fine report of the first barge to use the canal;

> 'At length in September 1763 the navigation between Lisburn and Belfast is complete. The first voyage was made by the Lord Hertford lighter of 60 tons with a cargo of coal, timber and other goods. The vessel belonged to Thomas Greg, a leading Belfast merchant, and his wife and he invited a large party to make the voyage and to dine on board. The principal gentlemen of Lisburn met the lighter at Drumbridge, a band played on board and a crowd of some thousand followed along the banks. The market square Lisburn was illuminated with lights at every window in honour of the occasion and there was a bonfire and barrels of ale provided by Mr Johnston, agent of the estate'.

The Lagan Canal had limited success, problems such as low water levels during the summer months restricting the size of cargoes. Water flows caused problems not only for the canal users but for the neighbouring landowners as maintaining the water levels in the canal slowed the run off and drainage from the adjoining land which was then subject to flooding.

The 19th century brought roads and road improvements and, with the arrival of the railways in the 1830s, the canal was facing increasing competition. The second railway in Ireland was between Belfast and Lisburn and opened in 1839. Rapid expansion to Lurgan, Portadown and beyond quickly followed. The junction out of Lisburn at Knockmore, with one line to Banbridge and Newcastle and the other to Crumlin and Antrim, opened a new world of better and speedier communications with a frequency that the canal could not match. However the Lagan Canal, despite its many handicaps, did provide a service to transporters of bulk items between Belfast and Lough Neagh which it continued to provide until 1958.

The 1798 rebellion by the United Irishmen did not have a great material effect on Lisburn though many of its citizens took part in the conflict in other areas. One such man was Henry Monroe who was to become the reluctant leader of the United Irishmen in County Down. Monroe was not a military man but a linen merchant who resided in the Market Square and worshiped in Lisburn Cathedral. He had not contemplated taking up arms against the King but had joined with the view that the excesses of the British Forces in the County Down countryside were intolerable.

Whatever his reasons, it was Monroe who led the forces of the United Irishmen at Saintfield where he defeated a British unit four days before the Battle of Ballynahinch. Monroe then moved to Ballynahinch with 7000 men where, on 13th June 1798, they joined in battle with the Crown forces under the command of General Nugent. They advanced along Dromore street in a flowing mass and Nugent, realising that he was being overwhelmed, ordered his bugler to sound retreat. The United Irishmen, unacquainted with bugle calls, mistook the call and retreated. Nugent, seeing the confusion, took advantage and routed the United Irishmen. Many were hunted down ferociously and Monroe was caught near Dromara. He was taken to Lisburn where he was hanged and beheaded and his head was set on a spike outside the Market House in view of his own home.

The 19th century saw further steady development of the town. In 1820 the new road to Hillsborough was opened with a new bridge over the River Lagan, which avoided the steep climb to the town up Bridge Street. 1837 saw the building of a dry dock in the barge basin just downstream from the Union Bridge. The dry dock was to help the users of the Lagan Navigation and, situated at a central position in the system, its building was a positive asset to the canal. The structure of the dry dock is still there although it was filled in when the road between Seymour Street and the Union Bridge was built.

Further improvements to the area were instigated by the inheriting of the South Antrim Estate by Sir Richard Wallace. The estate had been firmly in the hands of the Conway family since Sir Fulk Conway had been granted it in 1609, but by the 19th century the Hertfords did not take an active part in running the estate and indeed rarely visited Lisburn, leaving the management in the hands of an agent, although they did enjoy the considerable income the estate generated. The 4th Marquis of Hertford lived mostly in Paris and London and was not married. It is believed that Richard Wallace was his son and when the 4th Marquis died in 1870 it was to him that he left all that was not entailed, including the South Antrim Estate and property in England and France.

Richard first visited the estate with his wife in 1872 and it is recorded that the local populace erected an arch in Market Square on which snowdrops were laid out to form the words 'Cead mile failte'. Although he was also an absentee landlord, he took considerably more interest in the estate than did his predecessors. Under his ownership many improvements, both material and social, were made to the estate and he is honoured to this day in many of the place names around Lisburn.

The industry of Lisburn expanded dramatically during this period. In particular spinning and weaving increased to provide employment for the town leading to great accumulation of wealth and power by a number of 'Linen Barons'. Typical of these were the Barbour family from Paisley in Scotland who, as merchants, had been buying yarn in Ulster for shipment back to the Clyde for manufacturing. John Barbour saw the inefficiencies in this and in 1784 bought Plantation House, (which, though somewhat altered, is still there) at Ballymullan and built his first threadworks nearby. When John Barbour died in 1823 his eldest son, also John, continued the business until his death in 1831 when William (the younger son who was established at Hilden) bought the Plantation business and merged the two plants into a single operation at Hilden. In time this business was to become the largest threadworks in the world.

Robert Stewart & Son also expanded during this period. A newspaper report of 1st February 1889 stated:-

> "Messers Robert Stewart & Sons, linen thread manufacturers, Lisburn have just completed the erection of a splendid new mill as an addition to their business premises. When finished, the mill will cost upwards of £30,000, and will give employment to some 250 or 300 hands, in addition to the 800 already employed by the firm........For artificial lighting the agent used is electricity, and it may be remarked that this is the first mill in Ireland which is lighted throughout in this manner. .....the sanitary arrangements are on the most approved and perfect principal with toilets on every floor."

The end of the century saw the beginning of consolidation as improvements in machinery reduced the numbers of those employed. The effects of changing world markets and ever-increasing technology could not be held back for long and, since the Second World War, there has been a vast reduction in the numbers of people employed in the spinning and weaving trades. Businesses that continue today have survived because they maintained investment in new machinery and techniques.

The changes in manufacturing technology were tremendous but the 20th century saw even greater changes in social conditions, with workers' housing and health-care now being incorporated as part of the overall picture. Today, as housing stock has been improved, Lisburn has very few examples left of the mill workers' houses built by the mill owners in the last century. It is worth remembering that although, by today's standards, the mill houses were cramped and uncomfortable, in their time they brought improvements that were unthinkable previously. Parallel improvements in transport and communication mean that today the independence of the town of Lisburn seems under threat. As Belfast spreads, and many of the people of Lisburn and District work in Belfast, it might appear that a question of identity has arisen.

However Lisburn retains its own identity. From 1660 until 1884 Lisburn had the right of electing its own Member of Parliament - an honour conferred on the town by Charles II because of its loyalty to the Crown. During all those years and ever since it has always returned men who have been in the Tory tradition. In this and in many other ways Lisburn's citizens remain distinct from the neighbouring city. When Lisburn welcomed Sir Richard and Lady Wallace in 1872 in Irish, it illustrated a tolerance in views that still holds true today.

Important Dates from Lisburn's Past

2500-2000 B.C. Construction of Giant's Ring Complex.

500 A.D.   Monastic settlements established from this date.

600   Raths and forts constructed.

1004   Brian Boru and his Army at Blaris.

1602   Edward Bruce, brother of Robert Bruce, at Blaris.

1609   Killutagh acquired by Sir Fulk Conway.

1622   St. Thomas' Church (Lisburn Cathedral) founded.

1624   Sir Fulk Conway died.

1627   Sir Edward Conway carried out improvements to castle.

1641   Lisburn attacked by Rebels and the battle of Lisnagarvey fought 28th November 1641.

1658   Jeremy Taylor (later Bishop) came to Lisnagarvey as chaplain to the Conway family.

1662   The Church of St. Thomas became the church of Lisburn alias Lisnagarvey, known as Christ Church Cathedral.
            Charter granted to Lisburn by Charles II.

1667   Bishop Jeremy Taylor died 13th August.

1689   Duke of Schomberg's army stayed in Lisburn and District.

1690   King William III stopped briefly in Lisburn 19th June.

1698   Louis Crommelin came to Lisburn.

1707   Lisburn accidentally destroyed by fire 20th April.

1763   Lagan Canal between Belfast and Lisburn completed.

1774	First Methodist Church.
1784	Barbour's threadworks established at the Plantation.
1794	Lagan Canal to Lough Neagh completed.
1798	United Irishmen Rebellion, Henry Munroe hanged in Lisburn.
1801	Alexander Turney Stewart born at Lissue, went on to build world's first department store in New York.
1839	Second railway in Ireland completed between Belfast and Lisburn. John Balance (later Prime Minister of New Zealand) born at Ballypitmave, Glenavy. General Mulholland born.
1842	Christ Church, Hillsborough Road opened.
1857	General John Nicholson killed in Delhi.
1863	Railway Street Presbyterian Church opened.
1872	Sir Richard Wallace became new landlord of South Antrim Estate.
1885	Thompson Memorial Home opened.
1890	Sir Richard Wallace died.
1914	World War I commenced.
1916	Battle of the Somme, many Lisburn men killed.
1939	N.I. military district HQ moved to Thiepval barracks.
1972	Lisburn Borough Council created from Lisburn Borough Council, Lisburn Rural District Council, Hillsborough Rural District Council and part of Moira Rural District Council.
1994	Linen Centre opened to celebrate and display the Linen Heritage in which Lisburn played a major role.

Jack Calderwood

Name and Address	*Telephone*

RAILWAY STREET

The railway line between Lisburn and Belfast opened in 1839 and was the second line in Ireland. Railway Street, which connects the station to The Market Square, was originally called Jackson's Lane and led to the town parks which were plots of 2-3 acres where some of the citizens of the town grazed cows and horses. Today the street is the site for several prominent buildings including the Friends Meeting House, Railway Street Presbyterian Church, Lisburn Orange Hall and the Library. Behind the eastern side buildings is a private garden which had its origins in the 17th century, a true rarity in Ireland.

With thanks to Richardson & Cardy

B

Name and Address	Telephone

D. S. CAMPBELL PHOTOGRAPHERS

At the corner of the Market Place and Chapel Hill, this attractive red brick building was once Thompson's grocers shop. Since then several businesses have been based here and it is now the photography studio of D. S. Campbell. The junction of Market Place, Chapel Hill and Bow Street is today a busy traffic junction but in the past it had occasional high days. Twice a year horse fairs were held in the town when horses were traded in Market Place and up Chapel Hill. Horses and ponies were trotted up and down past this building to the shouts, cheers and laughs of the crowd. Today David Campbell's award-winning portraiture records that which will be tomorrow's history.

With thanks to D.S. Campbell Photography

Name and Address	*Telephone*

THE RAILWAY STATION

The Ulster Railway began operations on 12th August, 1839. Next day's Belfast News Letter reported that the average journey time was between 15 and 19 minutes, but could have been faster "had it been desired". The report went on,"...the train continued to fly up and down each alternate hour during the day until 8 o'clock in the evening as had been previously arranged ...... the crowds assembled in the neighbourhood of the railway were immense, and universal enthusiasm prevailed at the success of the undertaking." The station of today is not the station the trains in 1839 left from or arrived at, but is the second station built to accommodate the growing needs of the town.

With thanks to P. J. Brogan Optometrists

Jack Calderwood

Name and Address	*Telephone*

THE METHODIST CHURCH

Many residents of Lisburn embraced Methodism during its early days when John Wesley was a frequent visitor to the town and preached to large audiences from the Market House. Its growth over 250 years has been steady and the present church in Seymour Street is the fourth which has had to be built due to increasing congregation sizes and needs. Built in 1875, at a cost of just over £4000, the church remains virtually unchanged today. When the present pipe organ was installed as a memorial to those who had served in the First World War it cost approximately £1400.

With thanks to Country Classics

Jack Calderwood.

Name and Address	Telephone

DUNEIGHT MOTTE

Over time Ireland has had many influences. Certainly the Old English, the Vikings, the Normans, the New English and smaller groups like the Huguenots left their mark, but it was the Normans who perhaps left the greatest legacy with their great castles like Carrickfergus and Carlingford as well as many smaller mottes and baileys dotted across the country. Built around 700 years ago, Duneight Motte, overlooking the Ravernet River, is a monument to the change that the Normans brought to the area which, in a different way, was repeated 400 years later when the Conways (themselves of Norman descent) acquired the great South Antrim Estate with Lisburn at its centre.

With thanks to Illuminari

Jack Calderwood.

Name and Address	Telephone

GATELODGE TO THE MANOR HOUSE

Built around 1855, No.1 Manor Drive has been absorbed into the urban scene, but remains a good example of the gatelodges attached to a number of large houses at the time. The Manor House of which this was the gatelodge was the residence of the Stannus family who were the Conways' agents in the mid-1800s, looking after the affairs of the estate. When Sir Richard Wallace took over the estate in 1872 he brought in the Capron family as his agents, but the Manor House remained in Stannus hands until 1933. For a time the Manor was owned by the church who used it as an orphanage until it was demolished in the 1980s to make way for sheltered accommodation.

With Thanks to McAlpine & Co.

Jack Calderwood

Name and Address	*Telephone*

CASTLE HOUSE

Castle House (or Wallace House) was completed by Sir Richard Wallace in 1880 to redeem a promise made in 1845 by the 4th Marquis of Hertford to his tenantry, to build a house in Lisburn. It is a most impressive house set back from the street with balancing buildings at street line on either side contributing an air of authority which, together with the planting of the Castle Gardens, provided a near perfect setting. The splendid woodwork and plaster work has been restored and today the house must look much as it did in 1880. It was acquired in 1914 for use as a Technical School, a function which, as Lisburn College of Further Education, it continues today.

With thanks to M. T. Doherty & Co. Solicitors

Jack Calderwood

Name and Address	*Telephone*

THATCHED COTTAGE, HILL HALL ROAD

This pleasant single-storey, white-washed cottage at the edge of Lisburn town is a good functional example of the type of dwelling which at one time was commonplace as home to generations of hard working people. Until twenty years ago there were many similar small thatched houses in Lisburn, but one by one they have fallen into decay as thatching has proved difficult due to a lack of proper straw and thatchers being as scarce as hens' teeth.

Bow Street up to the 1930s had a number of thatched houses and shops, some of which were two storeys tall. In the Ballinderry and Moira areas there are still several examples of two-storey thatched houses in the English style.

With thanks to Knox & Clayton, Architects

Name and Address	Telephone

BARBOUR CAMPBELL THREADS

John Barbour was a Scot from Paisley who came to Ulster in the late 18th century to buy linen yarn for Scottish manufacturers. He found in Ulster a land where flax grew in abundance and spinning and weaving were established industries. He set up his original factory in 1784 at The Plantation but, in 1812, his son William moved to the present site at Hilden to found William Barbour & Sons, soon to become the world's largest linen thread producers. Further generations expanded the business world-wide and, though it passed from Barbour hands in 1978, so it has remained. Today Hilden exports to over 135 countries, continuing 200 years of domination in thread manufacturing.

With thanks to Barbour Campbell Threads Ltd.

Jack Calderwood

Name and Address	Telephone

'WALLACE' DRINKING FOUNTAIN

Richard Wallace first rose to fame during the siege of Paris in 1870-1871. Living and working in Paris at the time, he was Chairman of the British Charitable Fund and also gave generously of his own funds for relief. When peace returned Wallace received public recognition of his work when he was awarded the Legion d'Honeur by the French and in 1871 Queen Victoria made him a baronet. On leaving, he presented fifty cast-iron drinking fountains (which became known as Wallaces) to the city, as a reminder of the value of drinking water during the siege. Some of these survive in Paris and two remain in Lisburn, one in The Market Square the other in the Castle Gardens.

With thanks to Smyth Patterson Ltd.

Jack Calderwood.

Name and Address	*Telephone*

BALLYMACBRENNAN SCHOOL

Prior to the 19th century formal education was effectively only available for the wealthy. For others, the early Sunday Schools generally provided a much wider syllabus than religious education and the time spent in attendance was much in excess of that seen today. It was also the churches who, for a large part of the 19th century, provided the buildings for schools, establishing an influence which many retain today. Ballymacbrennan was a typical example of a country school from this period but the advent of improved transportation, allowing schools to extend their catchment areas, meant that many of these small schools were absorbed into larger ones who provided a wider curriculum.

With thanks to J. R. McKee & Co. Chartered Accountants

Name and Address	Telephone

DUNCAN'S DAM

For many years Lisburn obtained its water supply from several small watercourses on the north side of the town. One such watercourse, rising in the townland of Magheralave, flowed down along the glaciated valley to the holding pond in Wallace Park and from there, by wooden pipes, it fed into the town. As the town grew and its water needs increased, the valley was dammed to create Duncan's Dam in early 1870s, however, its position in relation to the growing town made it difficult to provide an adequate supply and in time Boomers Reservoir at Pond Park replaced it. Today the water level in the dam has been reduced and the area landscaped to form a delightful park.

With thanks to Boxmore Plastics Ltd. Composites Division

Jack Calderwood.

Name and Address	*Telephone*

CHRIST CHURCH CATHEDRAL

The original church, called St. Thomas' and referred to as a chapelry, was built by the Conways on this site in 1623. It was destroyed in the Rebellion of 1641, although the register was saved and is still in the Cathedral today. At that time the main church in the area was at Blaris but, as Lisburn began to grow around the Castle, it was St. Thomas' that became the principal place of worship. In 1662 the Charter of King Charles II formalised the matter when St. Thomas', then referred to as "The Church of Lisburne, alias Lisnagarvie," was constituted "To be forever hereafter the Cathedral Church and Episcopal Seat of the aforesaid several bishoprics of Down and Connor."

With thanks to S. Rankin & Co. Insurance Brokers

Jack Calderwood.

Name and Address   Telephone

THE TOTEM POLE

Today the well-known Forte Posthouse Hotel, this site was once the home of the Barbour family who owned Wm. Barbour & Sons of Hilden. Linen thread was the backbone of the business but, in slump periods and lean times, manufacture of flax fishing nets helped to carry the business over. The valuable Pacific salmon and rainbow trout fisheries of western Canada and the north western United States were valuable markets for Barbour nets. It was on a visit to western Canada in 1935 to encourage this trade, that Sir Milne Barbour acquired the Totem Pole from the Canadian Pacific Indians and he set it up in the grounds of Conway House where it remains to this day.

With thanks to Forte Posthouse Belfast

Name and Address	Telephone

MARKET DAY

Originally held in The Market Square, today the market has moved to Smithfield where it continues every Tuesday as granted by Charles I to Edward, Viscount Conway of Killutagh in 1628. Over the years the character of the Market has changed and the livestock and bulk farm crops have disappeared as have the old stalls which were wheeled from the Butter and Egg Market each market day and wheeled back again in the evening. They have been replaced with the huge variety of stalls to be found in any modern town market and perhaps the only thing that has continued through time is the presence of those who preach the Christian faith to the busy shoppers.

With thanks to Bow Street Mall Merchants Association

Welcome To
BROOKHALL HISTORICAL FARM

Jack Calderwood.

Name and Address	Telephone

BROOKHALL HISTORICAL FARM

Brookhall Historical Farm has, as part of its fabric, the former Parish Church of Magheragall (Ecclesia De Drumcale) which has a traceable history of at least 800 years. Part of the present dwelling adjacent to the former church is believed to be at least 400 years old, being part of a fortified house built by Sir Fulk Conway as part of the settlement of the South Antrim Estate. The site is being sympathetically restored by Mr and Mrs Johnston who have also put on view an extensive collection of Victorian farm implements and other historical artefacts which, together with the site's fascinating history and old-fashioned tea room, make a visit to Brookhall Historical Farm a most interesting excursion.

With thanks to Brookhall Historical Farm

Jack Calderwood

Name and Address	Telephone

LISBURN CASTLE GATEWAY

It is often quoted that the castle that stood on the site of the Castle Gardens was built by Sir Fulk Conway and begun in 1622. However, earlier chroniclers state that before Conway's time a castle belonging to the O'Neills (whose lands were taken by the Crown and given to Conway) existed on the site. This castle was described as "very imposing" and "consisting of an immense pile of buildings ..... seemed rather like some place of defence rather than the home of an Irish Prince". What Conway did was to improve and make the interior more comfortable. The castle was destroyed in the fire of 1707 and all that remains today is the Gateway, a reminder of a turbulent past.

With thanks to Lisburn Borough Council

Name and Address   Telephone

Name and Address	Telephone

CLONMORE HOUSE, HARMONY HILL ARTS CENTRE

Harmony Hill Arts Centre, as it is now known, looks down and across at the ancient townland of Clonmore, whose eastern boundary was the River Lagan and northern boundary Lambeg. As the area developed, Clonmore was absorbed into the townlands of Lambeg North and Lambeg South. However the Clonmore name lives on in the name of the house, built about 1905 by the Reade family. Passing later to another linen family, the Gordons, it was subsequently purchased for use as offices by Lisburn Rural District Council. When Local Government was reorganised it remained in the hands of the expanded Lisburn Borough Council and is presently used as an Arts Centre.

With thanks to Lisburn Borough Council

Jack Calderwood.

Name and Address	Telephone

THE UNION BRIDGE

Situated a little way downstream, the first bridge across the river at Lisburn carried the road from Carrickfergus and Belfast on its way to the steep hill at Bridge Street leading into The Market Square. The construction of the Lagan Canal in 1763 necessitated a new bridge which provided the crossing until the 1880s when it was replaced by the present Union Bridge in 1884. The lanterns on each corner of the bridge were cast at the Belfast foundry owned by the Musgrave family from Lisburn. At a time when business did not look further than local markets the Musgrave foundry had branches in Europe thus setting a trend as one of the first 'multi-nationals'.

With thanks to Greens Food Fare

Name and Address	Telephone

CHAPEL HILL

Bow House in Bow Street facing Antrim Street was the site of the Mass House, an early place of worship for the Roman Catholic community in Lisburn. As the community grew a new church was needed and this was built on the present site in 1794 and served until the end of the 19th century. Today's church was completed in 1903, but the spire was not added until 1933. The exterior is a little disconcerting due to the use of different building materials within two building periods. The church has a very dignified Romanesque interior and attractive full length statues of Saints Columbanus and Malachy are placed either side of the East Window.

With thanks to T & B Hague

Jack Calderwood

Name and Address	*Telephone*

LAMBEG

The meaning of the name Lambeg is uncertain as there are three possible derivations: little church, little arm and little hand. It is generally agreed that little church is the preferable explanation. Lambeg village was built around 1676 and Lambeg Fairs held on Midsummer's Day were great occasions in the village life. Reference has been found to horse-racing at Sandy Lane, Tullynacross as early as 1666. The establishment of the woollen industry by the Wolfenden family and later the bleachworks at Lambeg and the linen manufacturing firms for cloth and thread at Lambeg and Hilden give the village a just claim to being the birth-place of the Ulster Linen Industry.

With thanks to Cairnmore Antiques

Name and Address

Telephone

FRIENDS SCHOOL

Friends School was founded in the late 18th century at a time when there was concern in the Society of Friends for the education of their young people. The building of a Quaker school in Lisburn was no doubt progressed by meetings in Dublin at the time, however the immediate cause of its foundation was John Handcock's bequest of £1000. The school has had a chequered history which has been bound up with the fortunes of the Society of Friends, but after successfully coming through the difficulties experienced by the Society in 19th and early 20th centuries the school saw tremendous growth in the 1950s in the numbers of attending pupils who now embrace all facets of society.

With thanks to Chitticks Men's and Ladies Fashions

Jack Calderwood.

Name and Address	Telephone

THE WALLACE MEMORIAL AND CRIMEA WAR TROPHY GUN

Overlooking the River Lagan from the Castle Gardens, these two memorials are linked by their close associations with 19th century Members of Parliament.

The Trophy Gun was captured from the Russians during the Crimean War and was presented to the town by Captain Henry Meynell R.N. Member of Parliament for Lisburn 1824-1847.

The Wallace Memorial is the town's memorial to Sir Richard Wallace, Member of Parliament for the town 1873-1885. More importantly he was proprietor of the great South Antrim Estate 1870-1890 of which the town of Lisburn was the centre.

With thanks to Frederick Thomas

Name and Address   Telephone

RAILWAY STREET PRESBYTERIAN CHURCH

In 1885 Railway Street welcomed its new minister the V. Rev. R. W. Hamilton. A native of Donegal, in his teens he had emigrated to America where he worked for A. T. Stewart, a native of Lisburn, and was soon earning $100 per week. At the age of 20 his life took a new turn and he returned to Ireland to become a Presbyterian minister in 1880. While in Lisburn he was wont to call at the houses of his flock on a Saturday night and, perhaps as a result of his observations on these visits, he founded the Temperance Institute in the town with the help of members of the Society of Friends. It was built and paid for in a little over two years and this fine building still stands today.

With thanks to Natural Health Products

Jack Calderwood

Name and Address	*Telephone*

THE RIVER LAGAN

Rising at Slieve Croob in the Dromara Hills, the Lagan was once the principal source of power and clean water for the mills and bleachgreens which were built at strategic sites along its 40 mile journey to Belfast. In 1753 the Irish House of Commons was petitioned to establish a navigational link between Belfast and Lough Neagh, running part-way along the Lagan. Construction began in 1756 and by 1763 had reached upstream of Lisburn. However, with increased competition from the railways and improved roads, the navigation never succeeded financially and the final closure took place quietly in 1958. The towpath between Lisburn and Stranmillis today provides a pleasant walk.

With thanks to We Framed It

Jack Calderwood

Name and Address	Telephone

THE MARKET HOUSE AND ASSEMBLY ROOM

The centre-piece of the town for over 300 years, this building was witness to fierce fighting in the market place during the Rebellion of 1641. Improved stability in the 18th century saw the Assembly Room on the upper floor become the focus of local social life with 'genteel assemblies' held every fortnight and a 'Great Ball' annually. The 19th century saw many changes as concerts, political meetings and dinners replaced 'genteel assemblies'. In the 1880s renovations by Sir Richard Wallace changed the style of the building from Georgian to Victorian Italianate and in 1979 it was further modified when it became home for the Lisburn Museum.

With thanks to Lisburn Borough Council

Local Directory
and Sponsors

We would like to take this opportunity to
express our thanks to the following businesses
and organisations without whose help and
support this book would not have
been possible.

Unless otherwise stated all address are in Lisburn (Telephone code 01846)

BUSINESS NAME AND ADDRESS	TEL	FAX
Antiques		
CAIRNMORE ANTIQUES		
39 LAMBEG ROAD	673115	
Architects		
KNOX & CLAYTON		
2A WALLACE AVENUE	674312	607600
Bar & Off Sales		
HAGUE'S		
36 CHAPEL HILL	663588	607776
Chartered Accountants		
J R MCKEE & CO		
32 HILLSBOROUGH ROAD	665697	604335
Complete House Furnishers		
SMYTH PATTERSON LTD		
18 MARKET SQUARE NORTH	662707/662700	601367
Estate Agents		
MCALPINE & CO		
10 RAILWAY STREET	661214	661314
Food Retailer		
GREENS FOOD FARE		
23-25 BOW STREET	662124	670579
Health Foods		
NATURAL HEALTH PRODUCTS		
11 RAILWAY STREET	662551	603373
Hotel		
FORTE POSTHOUSE BELFAST		
300 KINGSWAY,		
DUNMURRY	(01232) 612101	626546

BUSINESS NAME AND ADDRESS	TEL	FAX
Insurance Brokers		
S RANKIN & CO		
21-23 BACHELORS WALK	676235	671289
Interior Artefacts, Gifts & Furnishings		
ILLUMINARI		
1 HASLEMS LANE (off Bow Street)	675675	
Kitchens & Bedrooms		
RICHARDSON & CARDY		
44A-48 RAILWAY STREET	678884	663509
Local Government		
LISBURN BOROUGH COUNCIL		
THE SQUARE, HILLSBOROUGH	682477	689016
Men's & Ladies Fashions		
CHITTICKS		
27-33 BOW STREET	662108	661337
Optometrist		
P J BROGAN AND PARTNERS		
79 BOW STREET	602020	
Outdoor & Country Clothing		
COUNTRY CLASSICS		
68 BOW STREET	603383	
Picture Framing		
WE FRAMED IT		
60A BOW STREET	607222	
63 ANN STREET, BELFAST	(01232) 240777	
Portrait Photographer		
D S CAMPBELL PHOTOGRAPHY		
2 MARKET PLACE	662742	662816
Prams & Nursery Toys		
FREDERICK THOMAS		
CASTLE BUILDINGS	665748	670334

CONT. OVER

BUSINESS NAME AND ADDRESS	TEL	FAX
Reinforced Plastics Manufacturer		
BOXMORE PLASTICS COMPOSITES DIVISION		
BLARIS INDUSTRIAL ESTATE,		
ALTONA ROAD	673312	607381
Sewing Thread Manufacturer		
BARBOUR CAMPBELL THREADS LTD		
HILDEN MILL	672231	678048
Shopping Centre		
BOW STREET MALL	675438	660342
Solicitors		
MELVYN T. DOHERTY & CO		
39 BOW STREET	674321	671430
Tourist Attraction		
BROOKHALL HISTORICAL FARM		
2 HORSE PARK, MAGHERAGALL	621712	

Open Diary

This section is provided to record personal
dates such as birthdays, anniversaries and
other important annual events.

January

1	16
2	17
3	18
4	19
5	20
6	21
7	22
8	23
9	24
10	25
11	26
12	27
13	28
14	29
15	30
	31

February

1 ....
2 ....
3 ....
4 ....
5 ....
6 ....
7 ....
8 ....
9 ....
10 ....
11 ....
12 ....
13 ....
14 ....
15 ....

16 ....
17 ....
18 ....
19 ....
20 ....
21 ....
22 ....
23 ....
24 ....
25 ....
26 ....
27 ....
28 ....
29 ....

March

1 ....   16 ....

2 ....   17 ....

3 ....   18 ....

4 ....   19 ....

5 ....   20 ....

6 ....   21 ....

7 ....   22 ....

8 ....   23 ....

9 ....   24 ....

10 ....   25 ....

11 ....   26 ....

12 ....   27 ....

13 ....   28 ....

14 ....   29 ....

15 ....   30 ....

                                                     31 ....

April

1	16
2	17
3	18
4	19
5	20
6	21
7	22
8	23
9	24
10	25
11	26
12	27
13	28
14	29
15	30

May

1	*16*
2	*17*
3	*18*
4	*19*
5	*20*
6	*21*
7	*22*
8	*23*
9	*24*
10	*25*
11	*26*
12	*27*
13	*28*
14	*29*
15	*30*
	31

June

1	16
2	17
3	18
4	19
5	20
6	21
7	22
8	23
9	24
10	25
11	26
12	27
13	28
14	29
15	30

July

1

2

3

4

5

6

7

8

9

10

11

12

13

14

15

16

17

18

19

20

21

22

23

24

25

26

27

28

29

30

31

August

1	*16*
2	*17*
3	*18*
4	*19*
5	*20*
6	*21*
7	*22*
8	*23*
9	*24*
10	*25*
11	*26*
12	*27*
13	*28*
14	*29*
15	*30*
	31

September

1	16
2	17
3	18
4	19
5	20
6	21
7	22
8	23
9	24
10	25
11	26
12	27
13	28
14	29
15	30

October

1	*16*
2	*17*
3	*18*
4	*19*
5	*20*
6	*21*
7	*22*
8	*23*
9	*24*
10	*25*
11	*26*
12	*27*
13	*28*
14	*29*
15	*30*
	31

November

1 ....

2 ....

3 ....

4 ....

5 ....

6 ....

7 ....

8 ....

9 ....

10 ....

11 ....

12 ....

13 ....

14 ....

15 ....

16 ....

17 ....

18 ....

19 ....

20 ....

21 ....

22 ....

23 ....

24 ....

25 ....

26 ....

27 ....

28 ....

29 ....

30 ....

December

1 ....

2 ....

3 ....

4 ....

5 ....

6 ....

7 ....

8 ....

9 ....

10 ....

11 ....

12 ....

13 ....

14 ....

15 ....

16 ....

17 ....

18 ....

19 ....

20 ....

21 ....

22 ....

23 ....

24 ....

25 ....

26 ....

27 ....

28 ....

29 ....

30 ....

31 ....

Cottage

Publications

Dear Reader

We hope you have found this book both enjoyable and useful. If you feel that it could have been improved in any way do please let us know.

This is just one of our range of illustrated titles. Other towns and areas currently featured include:–

Ballycastle and the Heart of the Glens
Ballymena
Ballymoney
Banbridge
Bangor
City of Derry
Coleraine and the Causeway Coast
Donaghadee
Hillsborough
Holywood
Larne and the Road to the Glens
Newry
Newtownards
Strangford Lough

If you require any further information please call or fax us on (01247) 883876, E-Mail us on cottage_publ@online.rednet.co.uk or write to:–

Cottage Publications
15 Ballyhay Road
Donaghadee, Co. Down
N. Ireland, BT21 0NG